To: Amy

Thank you for
coming to SHRM 2021!

Karen Michael

STAY
HIRED

Thriving & Surviving in
the 21st Century Workplace

Karen Michael, Esq.

STONY POINT
MEDIA

Stay Hired / Thriving & Surviving in the 21st Century Workplace
Published by Stony Point Media
North Chesterfield, VA

Hardcover ISBN: 978-0-578-91072-7
BUSINESS & ECONOMICS / Careers / General

Images courtesy of Freepik.com (macrovector, jemastock, rawpixel.com, pch. vector, pikisuperstar, stories, studiogstock, johndory, iconicbestiary, vector-juice, katemangostar)

QUANTITY PURCHASES: Schools, companies, professional groups, clubs, and other organizations may qualify for special terms when ordering quantities of this title. For information, email StayHired@StayHired.net.

STONY POINT
MEDIA

Contents

You Got a JOB!
Now Let's Stay Hired!

You got hired!

This is what you have been pursuing your whole life—this moment in time is when you begin your work life.

I have worked in the area of employment law and human resources for almost three decades, and I've worked with all types of employers, listening and consulting with them about their employees. Organizations agonize over employment decisions because they recognize how important the new relationship is to the organization and the employee.

Imagine that in a sea of candidates, you stood out. This organization picked Y-O-U!

The organization sees you as that person who will add value. It wants you to be successful. Your success is the organization's success.

Employers rarely look to terminate an employee due to lack of skill or training. It's typically other things like attendance, attitude, motivation, or ethics that cause the employer to have no choice but to terminate an otherwise good and valued individual.

I don't want that to happen to you! You've worked too hard to get to this point. I want you to STAY HIRED, not fired!

! Start your job with a great attitude, knowing this is an exciting opportunity to show what you can do. This might not be your dream job. That's OK.

Every experience leads to a new learning opportunity for growth. This is the start—not the end—of your career.

If you are starting a job from college, high school, or trade school, there are several ways work is different from your educational experiences, so you might need to make some adjustments in how you approach it. The following are some examples of how work is different from college or trade school and, in some cases, high school.

At work:

- You are being paid to do a job, unlike in college or trade school where you paid to get an education.
- Performance matters. Unlike in school where you could show up for your 8:00 a.m. history class and occasionally doze off while listening to the professor or not pay attention, at work you need to be attentive and give 100% each and every day.
- You don't control your schedule. For example, you likely can't arrange to only work on Tuesday and Thursday like you may have in school. Your new employer sets the schedule based on the employer's needs.
- You can't just skip work like you could a class.
- You don't get to choose your assignments like you did your classes.
- You don't get to choose your manager like you did your professors.
- You will have little free time while at work during the day. There aren't study halls.
- You need to manage your vacation schedule. You no longer have summers off and two to four weeks off during the winter, but will likely have flexibility to choose when you use your paid time off, so planning will be critical.
- Your words and actions are now governed by a lot of **federal** and **state laws**.
- Your employer gets to dictate how you dress and how you groom yourself with few exceptions.
- What you say on social media could get you fired.

- You must resolve conflicts with your peers. You can't just avoid them on campus. You might have to work with them every day.

These sentiments are not meant to discourage you. Getting the chance to finally show off all you have learned and worked for is going to be exciting and energizing. These observations are designed to set up realistic expectations so that you can enjoy the same success in your work life as you have in your student life.

> **!** If you learn to be flexible and adapt to the working world, you will transition easily and begin a long and remarkable career in your chosen field.

At-Will Employment

Unless you enter into a written contract with your employer, most states recognize what is called at-will employment.

This means your employer can fire you for any reason or no reason at any time with limited notice, as long as it is not an illegal reason, such as discrimination or harassment.

Likewise, **you have the right to quit at any time,** for any reason at any time with limited notice. The relationship is mutual.

Every day in your work life
is a new day.

Your employer can change your job duties, change your schedule, and/or change your pay (going forward). If you don't like these changes, you can either work with your employer to make adjustments or search for another job and then resign after you have found another job.

Tips:

- If you don't like your job, work harder than ever to try to make it better.

- If you really, really despise your job, start searching for another job. But do not stop working hard. Always give 100% when working for an employer.

- Don't quit your current job until you have a new job. Avoid an unexplained gap in employment, if possible.

- Don't burn a bridge with your current employer. While you have the "right" to quit without notice, avoid doing so, if possible. Give your current employer two-weeks' notice that you are planning to leave. Send a polite resignation letter and thank your employer and supervisor. Leave on good, positive terms.

- Take nothing with you when you leave. Don't steal company information or electronic documents.

- If you get fired unexpectedly, take the high road. Don't yell or complain. Ask if you can resign in lieu of termination. By resigning, you can honestly attribute your reason for leaving to resignation when you apply to other jobs. Note, however, that a voluntary resignation may impact your right to collect unemployment benefits.

- No matter what happens, remain professional and keep your dignity.

- Work harder on your last day than you did on your first. Don't "RIP" (resign in place).

- Don't bad-mouth your employer to colleagues or to a new or prospective employer on your way out (including online).

CASE STUDY

Fred has worked for ABC Company for one year. He hates his job and his boss. He finds another job and walks out of his current job without notice.

Six months later, his old boss starts work at his new company.

Karma is not your friend.
Don't leave on bad terms
or burn bridges.

Introductory Period

Most organizations have an "introductory period" or "probationary period" ranging from 30 days to one year.

At the conclusion of this period, you should not assume you are out of the woods and cannot be fired.

Typically, employees are held to stricter standards during the introductory period, but even after it is over, the "at-will" employment rule will likely still apply .

10 Characteristics of a Successful Employee

1 Flexible and Adaptable—You may have been hired to do a job, but the needs of your organization may change quickly and often. Avoid the phrase, "It's not in my job description." Demonstrate you can adjust to the needs of your manager and company quickly and with little debate or conflict.

2 Cooperative—Get along with other people and train your attitude to get to "yes." Avoid being disruptive, difficult, or snarky.

3 Self-Motivated—Find ways to add value without waiting for someone to tell you what to do. See a need —fill a need.

4 Respectful—This includes everyone from the CEO to the person who picks up your trash. Everyone deserves respect. Never become aggressive, disruptive, or unprofessional. Never ever discriminate against or harass another person. Diversity is the strength of every organization.

5 Open-Minded—You might have learned to do something a certain way in trade school, high school, college, or prior job, but this organization might approach the job differently. Always offer suggestions on ways things can be done differently, but also consider that there might be alternatives. This is part of the give and take of what makes diverse organizations thrive.

6 Positive Communications—Engage often. In meetings, speak up, ask questions, and offer suggestions. Avoid negative communications such as gossip, and stay away from the drama that creates toxic work environments.

7 **Outstanding Customer Service**—Whether to a client or coworker, always make sure those who interact with you at work will receive an excellent experience in your interaction. This is how you will build your positive reputation around the organization and with clients.

8 **Accountable**—You are going to make a mistake, probably many of them. Always own up to them—right away. Don't try to hide it or cover it up as tempting as that may be. And if you made a mistake, don't blame other people.

9 **Honest**—Be trustworthy. Always work with the highest level of integrity.

10 **Work Like an Owner**—You might not own the place, but treat your job like you do.

Payday Life

The good news is that unlike college where you were paying, now you are getting paid!

It's tempting when earning money to spend, spend, spend. Most people have already worked summer jobs and realize what they think they should be earning is not what is in the final paycheck. This is especially true with a full-time job, where the employer will likely deduct for insurance and other taxes.

If your employer has a 401K or some other savings plan, sign up for it immediately.

Once you set your spending lifestyle, it's hard to change. Learn to live with less early on.

Try to also have some of your paycheck go into a separate savings account to use for vacations, charitable giving, and/or emergencies. You will always feel that if you just earned a little more money, you would be fine.

Learn to live with what you have.

! Once you start working full-time, you will be offered the opportunity to live way beyond your means. Car dealers will loan you a lot of money for a new car, even if you make very little. Credit card companies will offer you credit cards with large balances, even if you earn very little.

Be careful! Live like you plan to live a really long time.

Enjoy the money you earn . . . go to dinner, buy a new car, but understand the limits of what you can afford and live accordingly.

Do Your Job

The best way to keep a job is to do your job. On time. As requested.

Even if the work you are going to be doing is difficult, boring, monotonous, dirty, exhausting, stressful, and/or not what drives you, put your whole heart and effort into this job and it will lead to other, even better, opportunities.

This is particularly true during your first few weeks of employment. Many times the training process is not exciting and sometimes flat-out miserable.

Orientation days are usually long and monotonous. Learning a new job can feel overwhelming.

It will get better if you set the tone early that:

- You care about your job.

- You take initiative.

- You are open to learning.

- You want to work hard.

Staying hired looks like this:

- When you're at work, work.

- Do what your manager tells you to do.

- Do the work on time.

- Be accountable for your work. Own your mistakes.

- Take initiative.

- Demonstrate a positive demeanor toward your manager and others.

! To make sure you are working when you are supposed to be working, your electronic device needs to be put away.

Do not get distracted by it or check it multiple times an hour, unless it is necessary for your job.

If you are at work and have nothing to do or have run out of productive work, consider what could be done to help your manager or employer, and then make the suggestion to him or her.

When you meet with your manager, come prepared with your list of suggested deliverables and how you plan to get them done. If a project or deliverable is delayed, tell your manager as soon as possible, and give an explanation. Don't delay giving your manager advanced notice that something isn't going as planned or expected.

When you make a mistake (and you will), tell your manager right away.

Showing value to your employer is the best way to keep your job.

! REMEMBER . . . it's the *choices* we make, not the *chances* we take that determine our destiny.

Every decision we make at work involving our own conduct is within our own control and can determine our professional destiny.

CASE STUDY

My first job at age 16 was working the ice cream bar at the Howard Johnson's off the highway. Wearing my brown-and-orange polyester dress, I scooped ice cream to weary truck drivers looking for a quick meal.

I needed the money, so I made sure I kept that job. I arrived for work on time and tried my very best to maintain a positive attitude toward my coworkers and customers.

One day, I was asked to serve in the main dining room. I still remember when a family left me a $5.00 tip on my first shift, which at that time was a lot of money and much more than expected.

That job wasn't what I wanted to do with my life, but it was what I was doing at the time and I did the job I was tasked with.

> There is value and dignity in every job, whether hospitality, retail, clerical, public safety, government, janitorial, construction, or professional. Showing respect to others in their work as well as self-respect for your job will help adjust any negative stereotypes you might have about your work.

CASE STUDY

Not excited by her new job at a pizza restaurant, a woman takes to Twitter and says, "Ew I start this f***ass job tomorrow," accompanied by seven thumbs-down emojis.

Her prospective employer sees the post and responds with his own Tweet telling her she does not start this "FA" job tomorrow because she is fired.

Obviously, that woman was not planning to have a good start of her new job. **This woman failed to be grateful to have a job,** which she apparently needed. With her negative perception of the job before she even arrived for her first day, her demeanor would have likely resulted in a very short career there.

Going into a job with negativity will likely yield negative results at work.

! Do your job with a good attitude, even if you don't like your job, until you find a new or better job.

Follow the Rules

On your first day or shortly thereafter, you will likely be provided either an employee handbook, a link to a site where policies are posted, or some other method of sharing the employer's expectations.

You will likely also be required to validate in some way that you have read and are familiar with these rules or policies.

You will be held accountable for these rules. While it's very boring to read a bunch of policies, you should be familiar with what is in them.

Policies may include expectations around:

- Social media use
- Confidentiality
- Conflict of interest
- Outside employment
- Drug and alcohol use
- Attendance
- Workplace conduct
- Workplace ethics
- Workplace violence
- Dress and appearance
- Computer usage and information technology
- Safety
- Criminal charges and convictions
- Introductory period
- Performance management and termination
- Harrassment and discrimination

Know them.
Comply with them.

Be on Time
for Work

The #1 complaint I hear from employers about employee performance is poor attendance.

If you plan to be early, then you will rarely be late. The best way to make sure you have on-time attendance is to develop a regular and consistent schedule during the workweek. An example follows:

- **6:30 a.m. to 7:30 a.m.:** Get up and get ready for work.

- **7:30 a.m.:** Commute.

- **8:00 a.m. to 5:00 p.m.:** Work.

- **5:30 p.m.:** Get home and/or work out.

- **6:30 p.m.:** Start dinner and eat.

- **7:30 p.m. to 9:30 p.m.:** Leisure time (video games, TV, read, etc.)

- **9:30 p.m.:** Get ready for bed.

- **10:00 p.m.:** Go to bed.

Straying from this schedule for activities like happy hour or late-night drinking will make it difficult to keep your schedule. Your employer will see where your priorities are if you come to work after being up until 2:00 a.m. drinking.

Work Time = Work Time   Off Days = Your Time

SIMULATION

To make sure you arrive on time for work, perform the following exercise. Assume your job starts at 8:00 a.m.

Here is where you should NOT be at 8:00 a.m.:

Leaving your house

On the highway

At the toll booth

In traffic

Pulling into the parking lot

In the parking lot

Entering the building

Going through security

Putting your makeup on or shaving in the bathroom

Talking with your coworker

Getting breakfast

Getting coffee

Smoking a cigarette

Here is where you should be at 8:00 a.m.:

At your work area with your computer turned on or at your workstation *ready to work.*

How to Get to Work on Time

Again, let's assume your work starts at 8:00 a.m. Let's also assume that before walking out of the door to leave for work, you:

- Are fully dressed
- Have all your makeup on and/or you have shaved
- Have eaten breakfast
- Have your coffee
- Have enough gas in your car to get to work

On a typical morning during the workweek, the commute is 25 minutes and:

- It takes five minutes to find parking.
- It takes five minutes to walk into the building.
- It takes five minutes to go through security and walk to your desk.

Build in another 10 minutes for unexpected traffic.

What time should you leave the house? If you chose anything other than 7:10 a.m. or earlier, you will be late to work and get fired. Not 7:11 a.m., not 7:12 a.m., not 7:15 a.m. Don't let time creep up on you. Never leave the house after 7:10 a.m., even if you find you are arriving a little early to work.

> The day you leave a little late is the day that there will be a backup on the highway.

CASE STUDY

Sally is consistently late. This morning, the manager plans to discipline her for her attendance, but she is late again.

As she comes into the meeting, she has a bag from McDonald's. This image sends the message to the employer that even though she was running late, she still managed to stop and get breakfast.

When the employer asks her about it, she says she has diabetes and could die if she did not eat breakfast. The employer correctly tells her that if her life depends on eating breakfast, she needs to get up earlier and leave earlier to build in time for breakfast.

! There is no excuse for her chronic tardiness.

Make no excuses.
Get to work on time.
Every. Single. Day.

While ideally you are never late to work, in reality, sometimes things happen. You will be late once in a while. If you build your reputation with your boss that you are reliable, your occasional (i.e. one to two times a year) tardiness will not impact your job. Just be sure to communicate with your boss right away when you know you will be late!

CASE STUDY

An employee sends his boss a text saying he is late due to a nail in a car tire. Because he is chronically late, the employer wants a picture of the tire.

The employee sends his boss a picture with a "nail" that appears to be in the tire, but on further review, the nail is photoshopped into the tire.

Don't be that employee
who is always late or
whose attendance has
to be constantly managed.

In addition to late arrivals, some employees show bad attendance by calling out "sick" frequently, especially on Fridays, Mondays, the day after the Super Bowl, the day after Thanksgiving, the day before vacation, the day after vacation, and other inconvenient times.

Some employees enjoy certain legal rights due to medical conditions to have sporadic attendance, and these are discussed in the "Your Rights at Work" section.

Be mindful of drinking too much the night before a workday. If you are going to a happy hour or out to dinner, consider how many drinks to consume so you are still able to give your full performance at work the following day.

> **!** Too often employees view sick days as freebies that can be used liberally. Chronic absenteeism puts a significant strain on your coworkers, manager, and organization. Last-minute notice makes planning very difficult. Only call out when you are truly sick or cannot come to work due to an unplanned emergency.

Build up your credibility and reputation for being a solid employee, and the occasional need to be absent will not be a problem.

In addition, many employees call out unnecessarily and then regret when they actually need time but none is left.

Virtual/Remote Work Attendance

As discussed more fully in the following "Virtual Work-place" section, after the 2020 pandemic, many employees began working remotely. **Some employees wrongly viewed this arrangement as an opportunity to avoid accountability.**

> **!** If you are so fortunate to be offered a telework arrangement either full-time or occasionally, you need to treat this arrangement as though you are on-site at work.

For example, if you are expected to be on a virtual call at 8:00 a.m., you need to do all the same planning as earlier, minus the commute, and log onto the call 5 minutes early. You may have trouble connecting, the link might not work, and/or you might not even be able to find the link.

Plan.
And be early.

> Be just as presentable for your virtual meetings as you would if you were going to the office.

If the call starts at 8:00 a.m., do not wait until 7:59 a.m. or 8:00 a.m. to initiate the call. If you do, you will be late.

Working remotely requires that you adhere to a full and regular schedule and be available, as requested and needed by your supervisors.

Your Boss Is Not Your Enemy. Your Boss Is Not Your Friend.

You likely have a boss who oversees your work. Sometimes this person is called your manager, supervisor, or leader.

This person should not be your best friend.

Don't become too familiar or friendly with your boss. Do not "friend" your boss on any social media platform other than LinkedIn.

Your boss is not your enemy.

Your boss does not hate you or want you fired. Your boss wants you to do your job on time and without drama.

If your boss gives you counseling, coaching, or discipline, this may mean your boss feels you are not doing something needed for success in your job. This also means your boss cares enough about your career to take the time to let you know.

In receiving this feedback, don't deflect or become angry, even if you disagree with how your boss describes the events leading to the discussion.

You should thank your boss and seek ways to improve.

Employees who become defensive every time a manager points out a performance or behavior weakness will not be successful.

Remember, your boss does not hate you or want you to fail.

In most cases, your boss hired you to do a job needed in the organization and is talking to you because he or she sincerely believes you are not fully meeting the needs of your position, either in conduct or performance.

Follow Management's Instructions

Throughout our lives, we have needed to follow someone else's instruction, whether it be a teacher, coach, or parent. Failure to comply with the instructions of people in authority likely resulted in negative consequences.

This same concept exists in the workplace. You may not like or respect your boss, but you need to do what he or she tells you to do when he or she tells you to do it, regardless of whether you agree with it or not (unless the request is illegal or unethical).

The following may be true, whether in reality or perception:

- Your manager is a jerk.

- Your manager is mean.

- Your manager doesn't know what he or she is doing.

- Your manager doesn't like you.

- Your manager is giving you busy work.

- Your manager is setting you up to fail.

- Your manager is asking you to do something meaningless.

None of that matters. You report to your manager because your organization has entrusted that person to accomplish something by, in part, using your talent.

What your manager says goes.

The exception, of course, is if you are asked to do something illegal, immoral, or unethical.

In those situations, you should seek guidance from human resources, your supervisor's boss, or someone else in authority.

CASE STUDY

Fred works for an organization where he has to keep track of his time on his calendar. He records the four hours he spent to complete his short-term disability paperwork.

His manager emails him, informing him that policy states this task is not considered work, and he must submit leave for those four hours. The employee is not familiar with the policy and asks for a copy.

The manager says there is not a written policy, but that he needs the leave slip by 5:00 p.m. that day. The employee responds that when he receives a copy of the policy, he will then send him the leave slip.

After 5:00 p.m., with no leave slip, the employee is disciplined. When he grieves it, the discipline is upheld **because he did not follow his manager's instructions.**

If the employee disagreed with the instruction, he should have sought guidance from the manager's manager or someone in human resources. **Ignoring the instruction was not an option.**

Most bosses have someone they report to or there is an opportunity to appeal a manager's decision.

However, avoid being that employee who complains about everything all the time.

As stated earlier, **your boss is not the enemy.**

CASE STUDY

A manager asks his employee to stop by his desk each day to check in upon arrival at work. The employee, who already exhibited a negative demeanor, refuses saying he feels like he is checking in with his parole officer. **This type of attitude cannot be tolerated in the workplace and does not support a healthy and cooperative work environment.**

! The #1 way to lose your job or hate your job is to create an antagonistic ● relationship with your boss.

When at Work, Actually Work

Repeat after me:

MY ELECTRONIC DEVICE NEEDS TO BE PUT AWAY DURING MY WORKING TIME.

I REPEAT!

MY ELECTRONIC DEVICE NEEDS TO BE PUT AWAY DURING MY WORKING TIME.

Being on your electronic device during meetings or while working is a huge distraction and a bad habit. It tells your employer you are not engaged.

CASE STUDY

You are in a virtual meeting. The big game is being broadcast from England. You have your phone in your lap with the game on. No one will notice. You have it on mute.

The meeting you are in is boring, anyway. You occasionally look down at your lap.

By doing so, you are showing that you do not care about your job and that you are too immature to pay attention to the work at hand.

CASE STUDY

Your friends from college are in a group chat. They are bored at work, too.

In between checking emails and doing your project, your phone is pinging because they are all conversing about the crazy time you guys had at that party.

This is not urgent, and by hanging onto your phone all day, **you are developing a bad habit** of not focusing on your job and demonstrating to your employer that you are not engaged.

> **!** Put the phone away! Make the decision to only check it every 30 minutes or once per hour, not every two seconds.

In addition, get off social media while working. These distractions show your employer that you are not interested or engaged.

Stay engaged while working.

CASE STUDY

Some employers have a policy that occasional social media use while at work or viewing personal emails will not violate company expectations.

The problem is that most people don't understand what "occasional" means and rely too heavily on the employer's assurance that occasional use is OK.

If your employer has such a policy, set a standard that you will not use social media during working time more than a total of 10 minutes during the day.

> **!** Keep in mind that when you are using social media or engaging in other personal activities when you are being paid to work, you are essentially stealing from your company.

You can use social media during your designated meal period and breaks, since that time is personal to you and not working time.

Leave the Drama at Home

Don't create, be the cause of, or be associated with workplace drama. **Your life problems are not the problems of your coworkers or your boss.** They are not the problems of your employer either, with the exception of legally protected rights afforded to you for the occasional things that happen and require an employer response.

Most employers want to help when they can and are empathetic to occasional life problems like the death or illness of family member, caregiving responsibilities, or similar concerns.

There is a difference between occasionally needing the support of your employer and being that employee with a never-ending cloud of misery and problems.

Here is a short list of the things that should **NOT** be discussed if happening all the time:

- Your car is broken down ... again.

- Your kid is in trouble at school ... again.

- You have that pain ... again.

- Your boyfriend/girlfriend broke up with you ... again.

- You are in trouble at work ... again.

- You are broke ... again.

People who bring drama into the workplace are the least liked employees by managers and coworkers. **Just because you might be miserable doesn't mean everyone wants to be miserable with you. They don't.**

Also, do not gossip about other people. It creates toxicity and disharmony with coworkers.

> Being that toxic employee who delights in everyone's misery will result in a short career at your organization.

CASE STUDY

If Constance doesn't have bad luck, she will have no luck at all. She comes to work miserable with another incidence of misfortune daily. The drama that surrounds her is never-ending. People avoid her and wonder how she can spend so much of the workday complaining, spreading rumors, and creating drama.

Don't be like Constance.

Toxic workplaces are caused
by people who create
toxic workplaces.

CASE STUDY

Alex is a real pain to be around. He has a major negative attitude, complains all the time, spreads rumors,
constantly talks bad about the company, his manager
and his job, and no one can stand to be around him.

Don't be like Alex.

Alex is a toxic co-worker.

How to Avoid Getting Sucked into a Toxic Coworker like Alex:

- Talk to your supervisor or HR about your concerns.

- Avoid people like Alex. Distance yourself.

- Don't be an enabler. Miserable people love talking about
  their misery and even more love being around other
  people who are miserable.

> Being around negative and unhappy
> toxic people will make you, and the
> workplace, more unhappy and toxic.

Ethics Matter

Assume you aren't going to get caught doing something illegal or unethical. Should you do it anyway? Should you steal? Falsify? Embellish?

All workers should develop an "ethics reflex," which is a process where they automatically make the decision to do what is right even if they aren't going to get caught.

> **!** Ethics reflex includes not just the big things (like embezzlement) but small things like taking company property to use later, using the company car for a personal errand, adding a few minutes to a lunch hour without reporting it, or using social media during working time.

These "small" things
can lead to termination.

Start your career with the decision that you will always avoid even the appearance of impropriety.

- Don't date a subordinate or your boss.
- Don't disclose confidential information.
- Don't falsify your timesheet or any record, and don't misuse company time.
- Don't take credit for the work of others.
- Don't take something that isn't yours.
- Tell the truth.
- Don't waste company assets (i.e.: taking a more expensive flight than necessary).

If you are doing anything in secret, don't do it.

! If you are worried what your mother, grandmother, father, jury of your peers, coworkers, etc. would think if they knew what you were doing, don't do it. *If it makes you think twice—think twice. Don't do it.*

Equity, Diversity, and Inclusion

Every employee brings rich diversity, including experience, education, and demographics. Organizations have worked proactively to encourage cultural additions to their workplace.

> The best and most successful organizations value the rich diversity each person brings to the workplace. They will do their best to include a person's unique characteristics to add value to the organization and to enrich each employee's experience.

As you enter the workplace, you should recognize that **every organization has organizational norms.** These norms form the workplace culture.

This doesn't mean that your diversity isn't valued—everything about you is unique and brings an important addition to the organization.

In 2020, an important renewed focus on the rights and needs of our Black population caused many employers to engage in the necessary dialogue to bring respect, fairness, and opportunity to the workforce. There was also important attention to the negativity toward Asian and Pacific Islander individuals following the 2020 pandemic.

> **!** **Diversity is more than race.** It encompasses our physical and mental abilities, age, gender, national origin, religion, sexual orientation, gender identity, education, prior experiences, parenting, and so many other characteristics.

We are not monolithic, so making assumptions about people can be troubling.

Most people will declare that they are expressly unbiased, but every one of us holds a set of unconscious biases that have formed over a lifetime. These biases are triggered, in most cases, without us even being aware of them.

As you enter the workplace, **engage in these dialogues with an open mind,** listen, review, and consider how your unconscious bias could be impacting your workplace relationships and decisions.

! It is critical that we all recognize our unconscious bias so that we do not articulate those or act upon them in the workplace or online.

Organizational norms may include on-time attendance, professional attire, communications, on-site interactions, teamwork, flexibility, integrity, and positive demeanor, among other expectations.

Even as you and your colleagues assimilate to organizational norms, everyone should strive to encourage individuality so that all our colleagues can feel a sense of belonging and inclusion.

CASE STUDY

Johnnie is a vegetarian and works with people who love to eat lunch at a local chicken place. Knowing Johnnie is a vegetarian, they invite him to lunch. **This is diversity.** Instead of going to the chicken place, they chose another place because it serves vegetarian food. **This is inclusion.** Johnnie is not just invited to lunch, but he can enjoy the meal.

We should all work to make sure that everyone can not only be invited to the table (i.e., hired to work at the organization), but also so they can enjoy the meal (i.e., fully engage and enjoy the work experience).

In some cases you have legal protections to show your individuality. For example, some state laws protect you from discrimination regarding your hair, including natural hair and certain ethnic hairstyles.

Virginia law, for example, prohibits discrimination "because of or on the basis of traits historically associated with race, including hair texture, hair type, and protective hairstyles, such as braids, locks, and twists."

Unless you have a religious objection, you should make every effort to assimilate into your organization by understanding the organizational norms and adapting to these norms with a good attitude and positive demeanor.

Some organizational cultures include drinking (and in fact, some companies offer beer trucks or happy hours). You should do your best to participate with coworkers but do not feel compelled to drink.

There are many reasons why people choose to avoid alcohol, including having a medical disability. **Don't feel like you have to make a big announcement that you don't drink,** you can simply attend the socials and bring your own nonalcoholic drink.

> **!** Assimilating to an organizational norm should not require that you do anything that violates your religion or ethical values. It also should not compel you to expose a disability or cause you medical harm.

Finding your place with a mentor

Whether you are in a minority group or not, sometimes just being new to a career or organization can feel out of place.

Some people in minority groups, or even those from certain schools or backgrounds, feel they have to prove themselves more than other people to fit in or be valued.

One of the best ways to grow and
develop is to find a mentor.
This isn't something that is
forced but naturally occurring.

Consider finding a mentor not necessary in your demo-
graphic or minority group.If you are a man – don't just seek
out other men to mentor you, and the same for women,
minorities, transgender, etc. **Seek out someone in
leadership who can help you develop and be
visible in the organization so your talents
can shine.** You need to show the leader that you are
motivated to succeed.

I'm amazed at how generous people are with their advice
if you ask for it.

When I was a young lawyer just graduating from law school I worked at a big prestigious firm with few women in leadership roles.

I was fortunate to have many male lawyers as my mentors, including the former CEO of Dominion Energy, Thomas Farrell, who passed away just before this book was published. He valued diverse talent and spent his career developing people to get them ready for their next level.

There are Tom Farrells in most organizations. You just need to find them, be open to the feedback, and show your appreciation for their efforts. **Be sure to not take too much of their time or abuse the relationship by relying upon them too much.**

> **!** Most mentors give advice and opportunity, and then expect you to **●** independently thrive.

Work-Life Balance

Sometimes it will feel you work all the time.
Many times people complain that, due to technology, we never stop working. You should view work/life balance like this:

Sometimes, work is a priority and you are going to miss something you wish you could do because of work.

Sometimes, other priorities (family, children, special interests) take priority over work.

The key is to know which takes priority and when. Organizations operate differently and you will learn the expectations of your job.

For most people starting a career, there will be long hours and hard work. **You should expect this.**

> You should try to enjoy weekends if you don't have to work and focus on things that are important to your life outside of work.

! Avoid gratuitous work that is either unnecessary or excessive. Check email only occasionally if that is important to your organization when you are not at work.

Try to avoid work showmanship. Producing good, efficient and high-quality work is more important that being available 24/7.

Virtual Workplace

During the 2020 Coronavirus pandemic, workplaces had to shift operations, and **many began relying upon employees to engage in a virtual workplace**, also known as "teleworking."

Some employees did this for a short period of time, and others were able to continue with the same arrangement long-term.

There are some jobs that can be performed full or part-time virtually, others simply cannot. If this is important to you, ask during the interview whether on-site attendance is an essential function of your job.

Telework requires excellent focus, initiative, and time management. It's easy to get distracted and to treat telework like a vacation. If you are permitted or required to telework, do the following:

- **Treat it like a normal workday.** As noted in the previous chapter on attendance, if your virtual meeting begins at 8:00 a.m., do not wait until 8:00 a.m. to log onto the meeting. Get to your workspace at least 15 minutes before the meeting to prepare, make sure you have the link, and log on. Be dressed and ready for the meeting and be early, not late, or just on time.

- **Make sure you have a safe work environment.** If you are injured in your home workspace and that injury arises out of the course of employment, you may be eligible for worker's compensation benefits.

- **Make sure your work environment is free from distractions.**

- **Keep your manager informed about what you plan to accomplish** when teleworking, and then let your manager know what you accomplished while teleworking.

- **Attend all meetings and don't be late.**

- **Be present with coworkers** as much as possible.

- **Dress appropriately** for all virtual meetings, and make sure your background is appropriate.

- **Respond in a timely way** to emails and other requests for information.

CASE STUDY

During the pandemic when court matters are held virtually, a Florida judge condemns lawyers and litigants for inappropriate attire and surroundings.

Participants had been attending meetings in their pajamas, from their beds, and one man was shirtless.

The judge reminds them that the Zoom hearings are hearings—not casual phone conversations.

Your virtual workplace
is still a workplace.

CASE STUDY

Early in the pandemic, television reporters are working remotely via Zoom. A reporter appears on television believing that only his top area is visible but actually, viewers can see his legs and observe that he is not wearing pants and is in his underwear.

CASE STUDY

As two female television morning show hosts are working from home using Zoom, they discuss their next guest, a male celebrity, and make sexually inappropriate comments about him. Unknown to them, the guest hears their conversation. He is understanding about it, but their actions are unacceptable.

Don't assume because you are working remotely that sexual harassment can't occur. It can and it does.

> **!** Voluntary telework arrangements can be revoked at any time unless telework is part of the job.

While employers were very understanding during the pandemic when an employee's six-month-old baby cried during the meeting, some employers may not tolerate ongoing childcare and other distractions during working time. Some employers have rules that an employee must have other child care while working from home. Be sure to check your employer's expectations.

In a telework environment,
you are no longer
working from home—
you are essentially
living at work.

Having a dedicated work area away from your common living space will help you separate work from living.

Avoid working all the time just because work is accessible all the time.

Set boundaries for yourself and expectations with your employer.

If you are nonexempt (paid hourly), be sure to keep accurate records for all time worked, and record them properly on any electronic timekeeping application. Your employer is not legally entitled to "free" work.

Resolve Conflict in a Respectful Manner

At work, **you will undoubtedly experience conflict** with a coworker, manager, customer, vendor, or someone you interact with. Working with the same people for eight or more hours each day could cause some disagreement. This is normal and healthy.

How you address these conflicts will determine your professional fate.

- Always be professional

- Never raise your voice

- Do not curse at anyone

- Do not become aggressive or belligerent

- Follow the chain of command

- Always be respectful

- Do not send an angry email or text message

- Do not resolve your conflict over social media

- Do not make a permanent or regrettable decision based on a temporary emotion

> **!** Disagreeable and difficult people will quickly develop a negative brand and impression of themselves and will likely not be considered a high performer by management.

6 Tips for Addressing Conflict at Work

1. Find the source of the conflict.

2. Meet in private to discuss it. Too often we let conflict fester until it reaches a boiling point.

3. Consider having a third party with you to help facilitate the conversation.

4. Listen—for real—to the other person

5. Determine if there is a middle ground—resolve what you can.

6. Move on. If you don't get your way, move on. You can't worry about things that are out of your control or can't change.

The best way to address conflict is to use empathy and consider the point of view of the other person. Then seek the win/win solution, where the conflict can be resolved with both people feeling as though they had some level of success in the conflict's resolution.

Be reasonable and flexible. Recognize when the conflict really matters and if it is worth the battle.

Dress Appropriately

Managers frequently complain about poor workplace attire. **Your employer has a right to set expectations** for appropriate workplace attire including clothes, jewelry, tattoos, and shoes.

! Your employer also has a right to set expectations that are different for men and women, as long as it does not cause a higher burden to either gender. However, your employer cannot implement gender stereotypes.

CASE STUDY

A female stereotype might be that women need to wear skirts. But if a woman wears a professional pant-suit, she should not be targeted because she is dressing more masculine, as long as her attire is consistent with the dress code.

Rule #1: If you can see up it, down it, or through it, DON'T wear it!

Rule #2: Flip-flops and crop tops are NOT okay in most workplaces.

Sometimes employees say they cannot afford a decent wardrobe. This is not an excuse. You can go to Target, Walmart, consignment stores, or Goodwill to find very nice and appropriate shoes or clothes. When you look in the mirror, ask yourself:

- Does what I am wearing comply with the employer's policy?

- If I have to wear a uniform, am I wearing it in a proper manner or have I sexed it up or tried to put my personal spin on it so it isn't compliant?

- Can I see up it, down it, or through it?

- Do I look like I am going clubbing?

- Are my shoulders showing too much?

- Can you see my midriff?

- Can you see my undergarments?

- Are my pants at my waist? Am I wearing a belt?

- Is my jewelry distracting?

- Do my tattoos comply with company policy?

- Is what I'm wearing too short? (Try the fingertip rule above your knee.)

- Does what I'm wearing fit properly? Is it too tight or too baggy? This includes pants, tops, and skirts.

- Are there holes in my clothing?

- Is the hem fraying?

- Are my shoes appropriate? Are they too old and worn?

- Does my attire portray the image the company wants?

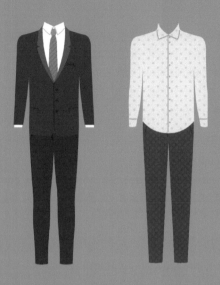

! If you want to know how to dress, wear what a person whose job you'd like to hold is wearing.

CASE STUDY

An employee seeks advice from a human resources (HR) columnist about attire counseling she received from her manager.

The employee says she wore "jeggings" (jeans that fit like leggings) to work and so did her best friend. Her manager stated that her attire was not appropriate while her friend's manager didn't say anything to her friend.

The columnist points out that the writer's manager cared enough about the employee's success that she took the time to explain to her about the inappropriate attire, while her friend's manager didn't care enough to let her friend know.

When you're dressing or grooming, consider what it says about you and whether it's in line with the message you want to communicate.

When a manager counsels an employee on workplace attire, the employee should thank the manager for his or her feedback, even if the employee disagrees.

Your appearance is your brand. When your manager counsels you, you are being advised that your positive brand in the workplace is being impacted. Perception is reality.

TIP: Don't wear it again.

!
The manager has the right to use his or her discretion in making a determination on workplace attire.

This discretion also may not be consistently applied in your workplace from manager to manager or department to department. So what? **Do what your manager tells you to do and move on.**

Groom Appropriately

You may technically meet the dress code requirement but still have other issues in your appearance.

> **!** Proper grooming includes having neat and clean hair, no negative body odor, clothes that are not disheveled, and generally a polished and professional look consistent with your organization's culture.

Additional considerations include extreme flatulence, odor from a person out drinking late, overbearing perfume or cologne, or the smell of smoke on someone's body/clothes.

What you wear is important, but **your overall appearance includes any distractions your presence may create.**

CASE STUDY

Sally works in a cubicle environment. She is a great coworker and employee who provides excellent customer service to her clients via phone. However, the manager has received several complaints about her body odor.

When her manager asks her if everything is OK and shares the concerns of her coworkers, Sally is embarrassed and says due to a medical condition, she has a difficult time with keeping herself free from odor.

Situations like this are awkward, but in an environment where people must work in close quarters, **everyone needs to respect others by maintaining a scent that is not unpleasant.**

CASE STUDY

Fred spends the night out drinking until 2:00 a.m. When he arrives at work at 8:00 a.m., he is disheveled and smells of alcohol.

When his manager approaches him, Fred states that although he stayed out late, he knows he needs to come to work on time. He admits he slept in his clothes.

Fred was not prioritizing his job, causing a lack of confidence in Fred's capabilities by the manager and his peers.

Before going to work, consider:

- Do I meet the dress code?

- Are my clothes wrinkled or full of pet hair? Picking up those black pants from the floor that the cat slept on all night is probably not the best choice.

- How do I smell? Covering up body odor with perfume/cologne is not a solution.

- Is my hair neat and clean?

- Are my nails neat and clean? Is my nail polish peeling off? Is there dirt under my nails?

- Are my tattoos offensive and if so, are they showing?

- Is my jewelry distracting?

Workplace Religious & Medical Accommodations

Sometimes people will groom based on a religious belief. The Equal Employment Opportunity Commission wrote about this here: **https://www.eeoc.gov/eeoc/publications/qa_religious_garb_grooming.cfm**.

If you have a sincerely held religious belief or medical condition requiring you to violate the company's standards for dress or grooming, **talk to your manager or human resources department** before the company addresses the violation with you.

> **!** You are not entitled to an accommodation unless you ask for one. Before you get disciplined for having a beard that violates company policy, seek out an accommodation.

The company does not have to provide a reasonable accommodation if the accommodation violates the organization's safety policy or health or safety regulations.

If your company states a safety or health reason why you cannot be accommodated, it's not personal. Your company will, however, need a legitimate and non-discriminatory reason to deny your accommodation request.

> *Just because something*
> *was done in the past does not*
> *mean it can continue*
> *into the future.*

In a recent case, a woman was required to wear steel-toed shoes for her job. However, she could not wear them due to diabetes and issues with her feet. Since wearing steel-toed shoes was a safety requirement, the court held she was not qualified for her job and could be terminated. Companies must always make safety a priority.

SAFETY ISSUE CASE STUDY

Employees in a correctional facility violate the uniform policy when they wear traditional Muslim headwear in support of their faith.

The correctional facility denies their request for an accommodation to wear the headwear due to safety concerns, such as hiding contraband, not being able to recognize the employee, and someone using the material from the headwear as a weapon.

The court upholds the correctional facility's decision to deny the request since it represents a legitimate safety concern.

RACE DISCRIMINATION CASE STUDY

Some African-American men suffer from a medical condition known as pseudofolliculitis barbae (PFB), which makes it painful to shave. In these cases, it may be discrimination for the employer to require that the employee complies with the grooming standards to be clean-shaven.

If the employer can demonstrate a uniformly applied rule that is an essential function to the position, the employee will likely fail to show discrimination. **The employee should talk to the employer about his needs** and ideally, find a compromise.

CASE STUDY

Samantha smokes cigarettes several times a day. Immediately after smoking by the door at the designated smoking area, she walks back into the building to her desk.

While she isn't smoking at her desk, the scent and odor from her cigarettes permeates the work area around her and even causes coworkers with allergies to become sick. Samantha is impacting others in her workplace by her actions.

Taking Time Off from Work

You will likely be entitled to paid-time off or some version of sick leave and/or vacation time.

! Always make every effort to plan your time off, and notify your manager in advance.

Be sensitive to the timing. For example, if at all possible, don't plan a vacation during the big software update if you are in IT.

On the other hand, if you have something special (like your best friend's wedding in Mexico), tell your manager immediately and ask for the time off even if the timing is not ideal.

> If you've built your reputation
> early with your employer,
> many times the request
> will be granted.

! Do not show up your first day and immediately start asking for vacation before you have eligibility.

Usually, **when you are new employee, you will not be entitled to time off immediately.** If you know ahead of time that you need time off before your eligibility kicks in, you need to **negotiate that during the recruitment process** before starting work.

Learn the expectations upfront.

- In some organizations, going entirely off the grid is expected during your time off.

- In other organizations, you are expected to maintain some contact (i.e. through emails).

- In some organizations, you are expected to all-out work, including being available for calls and other work while taking time off.

The latter is not ideal, but **understanding what is expected is important.** In this case, you might want to assess if this is a company you want to work for long term.

If you have time available, take it. In some organizations there is a "use or lose" policy, meaning if you don't take all your time off, you can't carry it over to the following year.

Taking time off is as important as working. You need to recharge. Take every minute of time off that the company provides.

Some organizations have a policy that allows unlimited time off. While this seems like an employee-friendly policy, the reality is that it sometimes creates guilt for employees who take time off.

If this is the case for your organization, test the waters to see how much time is typically acceptable. **A good rule is about three weeks, in addition to holidays.**

If you are on vacation and for whatever reason you cannot return as planned, notify your manager immediately and give an honest reason why you are not returning on time.

During the holidays, most people seek additional time off. Managers will usually prioritize time off approvals based on tenure.

This may result in your request for time off over the holidays being denied for the first couple of years, so plan accordingly. If your request for time off is denied, do not call out sick unless there is a true emergency. If you do call out sick, you will likely be required to provide a doctor's note.

Do Not Commit Harassment or Discrimination

Discrimination occurs when someone is treated differently, or less favorably, due to a protected characteristic, such as race or gender.

Harassment is a form of employment discrimination.

Harassment is unwelcome conduct based on someone's protected characteristic, such as race, disability and others mentioned, resulting in a hostile work environment for the individual.

Most people who are harassed at work don't complain. They just put up with it and/or quit.

Merely because someone is smiling and not expressing objection doesn't mean the person is consenting.

> **!** Don't harass or discriminate against your peer, customer, or anyone associated with your job.

Based on federal law, inappropriate harassment/discrimination occurs when conduct is based on:

- Sex
- Age (40 and over)
- Disability
- Religion
- National origin
- Color

- Race
- Sexual orientation
- Gender identity
- Genetic predisposition
- Veteran status
- Pregnancy

Your employer or state law may include additional protected characteristics.

Sometimes harassment is difficult to identify

because there might be confusion on whether the conduct is consensual or welcome.

To avoid the potential that you could be engaging in behavior that would violate the company's harassment policy, you should follow the list of "never evers" in the workplace provided on the next page.

"Never ever" do any of the following:

- Engage in any sexual behaviors

- Disparage another person's race or engage in racially disparaging conduct

- Disparage a person's medical condition or use the word "ret**d" toward someone

- Disparage someone's religion

- Make age comments like "over the hill"

- Bully another person or engage in verbal abuse

- Engage in conduct that is "anti" any of the protected characteristics

- Touch (as is outlined in the next chapter)

- Use a racial slur of any kind, whether it's for the same race or opposite race

- Engage in a sexual relationship with a supervisor or subordinate

Inappropriate sexual behaviors include the following:

- Requests for sexual favors

- Sexual activity or innuendo

- Sex-oriented kidding or teasing

- Inappropriate jokes

- Flirting, advances, or propositions

- Nicknames or terms of endearment (i.e., honey, sweetie, baby, dear)

- Comments about a person's appearance, clothing, or body, including creepy compliments

- Comments about a person's sex life

- Displaying sexually suggestive objects or pictures

- Creepy conduct, such as lurking, staring, glaring, or making unwanted statements that are too familiar and personal

- Exposing images of private parts or undergarments (including texting, snapchatting, or any form of electronic communication)

- Crude or obscene language

- Comments reflecting stereotypes

- Conduct that is too familiar or affectionate (i.e., texting someone with nonwork-related questions, such as, "What are you doing?' or "What's up?"; sending unwanted Facebook messages or Twitter DMs)

- Displaying offensive images either electronically, or in posters, art, cartoons, notes, photos, or pictures

- Watching porn while at work, even if on a personal device

Never engage in any of the identified conduct with a peer, even if it is between two people of the same race/sex/ national origin, etc. and even if you think it is consensual.

> **!** If you "never ever" engage in any of these behaviors with a colleague or anyone associated with your work, you will "never ever" have to worry about being accused of illegal harassment.

Some behaviors might not fall into the "never ever" list but are risky behaviors that could lead to misunderstanding or claims of harassment.

Risky behaviors are unlike the "never evers" because they could be welcome and thus not offensive or violate your company's policy, but the behaviors could potentially lead to a claim of harassment.

Risky behaviors include the following:

- Hugging (Consider putting this on your "never ever" list. Refer to the next section on touching.)

- Coworker dating

- After-hours socializing with co-workers

- Politics

- Cursing

- Compliments that are seemingly innocent between good friends

- Becoming too close emotionally and thus, crossing boundaries

- Horseplay

- Pranks

Harassment can be committed between coworkers and managers or by vendors, visitors, customers, interns, and contractors.

The sitcom "The Office" was fun to watch but the behaviors of those employees should not be replicated in any real workplace.

You have a right **to go to work and not experience harassment from anyone.**

CASE STUDY

A server at a restaurant waits on a group of individuals who engage in disrespectful conduct, including calling the server dear, honey, sweetie, and making comments to her about her appearance.

She wrongly believes she has to tolerate this conduct because she works at an establishment where alcohol is served. She doesn't. **She has a right to go to work and not be harassed** by customers.

In a perfect scenario, she tells the manager who advises the customers to leave or stop the unwanted conduct. Of course, the employee may feel this might impact her overall compensation because she will lose tips in order to end the harassment.

However, society needs to understand you cannot harass an employee in his or her job based on sex, race, etc.

CASE STUDY

You are interacting with a coworker via text message about a work issue. It's late at night and the conversation turns personal.

You then say, "You're beautiful, btw." The coworker doesn't respond.

You then say, "I hope you know how beautiful you are." The coworker responds, "Ha ha."

You have now creeped out your coworker.

This can lead to a claim of sexual harassment, even though it was done after hours.

No double standards: In some ways, society has created a double standard where men are held to a different standard for sexual behaviors.

Women should not be engaging in sexual behaviors and should also comply with the "never evers." There can be no double standards. Men and women must respect one another.

Regardless of who initiates it, sexual misconduct cannot be tolerated.

The "I didn't mean it" defense: Just because you don't intend to create a hostile environment for someone doesn't mean you can't be guilty of harassment.

For example, sometimes a coworker will engage in sexual banter with another coworker because she/he wants to date the other person, not engage in sexual harassment.

The intent doesn't matter. It's the conduct that matters.

If the conduct is unwelcome, you might lose your job, your reputation, your livelihood, and cause another person significant distress for your own personal gratification. It's not worth it.

Speak up: If you observe or are made aware of harassment in the workplace, you need to tell someone.

Talk to human resources, your manager, or someone in senior management. The law does not require that you speak to the offending party before making a complaint.

**Management will have an
obligation to take action
to end the harassment.**

Many victims do not bring these issues forward because they don't want the person to get in trouble or get fired.

You cannot control that, and the alternative is for the person to continue with the misconduct and then other people are impacted. **Unreported or unaddressed behaviors tend to escalate.**

! *You have a right* to be free from retaliation for engaging in what is called "protected activity," which includes raising a concern about harassment or discrimination or participating in an investigation into harassment or discrimination.

Federal law, some state laws, and most employer policies give you the right to raise a concern about harassment and discrimination and be free from suffering any form of retaliation.

The Bank: Normally, making a deposit in a bank is considered a good thing. But for a minute, consider your coworker has a special work bank that has a long memory.

You think you and your coworker have a good working relationship, so you relax your conduct and violate several "never evers."

The coworker is always smiling and laughing, so it doesn't occur to you that this could be a problem, until one day the coworker feels you have gone too far or the coworker gets upset with the organization or you personally.

Each time you violated the "never evers" with that coworker, you made a deposit in that person's work bank. **Now that you've gone too far, the person is ready to make withdrawals—lots of them.**

All the "never evers" you engaged in over the years that you wrongly believed were consensual are now being presented as offensive and unwelcome.

> **!** No matter how friendly and open a person appears, don't make a "deposit" in that person's bank—this includes sexual comments, racist or sexual orientation jokes, etc.

No deposits—no withdrawals.

Don't Touch Anyone

The person below is your coworker. Draw a circle around all parts of the body where you **CAN** and/or **SHOULD** touch him or her.

If you circled the hands, you may be right. Generally, the following have been accepted:

- Handshake
- High-five
- Fist pump

All of those are OK unless done excessively or with a creepy gesture, although there are cases when these behaviors seem inappropriate.

Any unwanted touching is a battery
—both civil and criminal—
in most states.

> **!** Battery is a criminal or civil offense that can be alleged following an unwanted/offensive touching. This typically happens when a person is touched without consent.

If you want to be sued personally and possibly go to jail (for one or more years), then touch someone. Otherwise, hands off!

It is *not* OK to do any of the following:

- Touch on the back
- Touch on the leg
- Brush up against anyone
- Massage someone
- Pinch someone
- Caress someone
- Touch a private area
- Touch someone's necklace or jewelry
- Touch someone's hair
- Do any touching other than a handshake, high-five, or fist/elbow pump

What about hugging? Some people like to hug at work, but not everyone wants to be hugged, and you probably can't tell the difference.

> As you start your career,
> make it a personal rule
> not to hug anyone at work.

Many people find it difficult and awkward to avoid a hug when someone approaches with arms wide open.

First, set the tone early in your career. When approaching someone for a greeting, you could reach your hand out to shake hands. After the 2020 pandemic, many people don't even want to do that.

If someone comes in for a hug and you are uncomfortable with it, decline it under the name of, "I'd hate to get you sick." You could also take a step back and put out your hand.

CASE STUDY

There is a sheriff in California who is accused of hugging his subordinate employee 100 times over a period of 12 to 14 years.

The employee says the hugs were sexual. The Sheriff says they were platonic, like he would give a grandma or a friend.

The case settles for $100,000. Divide 100 into $100,000 and **the going rate for a hug is $1,000.**

If you are prepared to write that check, then keep hugging. Otherwise, take it off your to-do list.

CASE STUDY

I trained a group of 300 employees on harassment pre-vention. During training, I used an interactive technology where participants voted on answers to a case study.

At the end of the training, one man stood up and com-plained that society was trying to change their culture.

He said he worked at the company for 25 years and everyone loved each other. He said they hugged and joked, and everyone was happy and no one was offended.

A participant in the back stood up and suggested I pre-pare a voting slide on whether they like to be hugged at work. I created a slide stating, "I like to be hugged at work." I told them to choose #1 for "yes" and #2 for "no."

89% of the participants said "no."

After seeing the results, I turned to the first man who spoke up and explained that of the 300 coworkers in the room, 33 said they liked to be hugged at work.

I asked him to identify who they were. He seemed con-fused by the question, saying there would be no way for him to know.

This is the point. **There is no way for you to know if someone agrees with the touching** or if it is truly consensual.

In this case study, the 25-year employee who spoke up liked to hug and be hugged. It made him feel good. However, other people deserve to work in a respectful environment. He was being selfish and doing what made him happy without thinking of others.

Perception is not always reality.
Most people go along to get along.

Here's the rule: **Hands off! Don't touch!**

A person is not required to tell you to stop or that the behavior is offensive before it is battery or leads to a successful claim of harassment. It is not the obligation of the victim to tell the perpetrator to stop. It is the obligation of the perpetrator to not engage in the behavior in the first place.

> **!** Before touching, ask yourself, "Is this worth it? Is this worth the end of my career, my freedom, my finances, and my reputation?"

Acts of Aggression and Threatening Behavior Have No Place at Work

Your employer does not have to tolerate threats, anger, an intimidating presence, or yelling.

- Don't make coworkers worry you will be the next active shooter.

- Don't make threatening statements.

- Don't brag about owning a gun.

- Don't be creepy, elusive, or strange.

- Don't threaten suicide.

- Don't make comments about harming your boss.

- Don't post things like, "Today you might not want to come to work."

- Don't slam doors, yell, shout, or throw objects at work.

- Don't "joke" about violent acts toward others.

If you are considering committing, or engaging in, any of the above, seek help. Even if you are kidding, you will likely lose your job. Employers cannot tolerate any acts of violence or aggression.

CASE STUDY

A long-term employee becomes increasingly disgruntled with her workplace. While she is an otherwise good employee, one day she comes to work and vocalizes a prayer to God that he prevent her from coming to work and shooting up the place. She then clarifies that her coworker is safe because she is talking about going "upstairs" where her managers work. This employee is terminated for making a violent threat even though it was unlikely she was going to carry through with it. She was probably just venting but her organization terminated her. The employer usually can't take the risk of keeping an employee who makes a threat, even as joke.

Texting, Sexting, Online Behaviors, and Electronic Communications

MYTH: What I say online cannot be used against me by my employer because I have a First Amendment right to say what I want.

MYTH: What I do after hours on my own time and on my own social media platforms cannot be used against me by my employer because it is my personal business done on my own time.

FACT: If what you do electronically impacts your ability to perform your job and interact with coworkers, then you can't work there anymore.

> ! Be careful what you put online, in text
> • messages, or in any electronic format.

FACT: The government cannot arrest you for posting racist, homophobic, or other inappropriate content online because **the First Amendment protects your right to express yourself.**

FACT: Your private employer is not the government.

> ! The First Amendment does not apply to
> • your private employer.

FACT: Even if you work for the public sector, your First Amendment rights are limited as it relates to your job.

> ! If your private online behavior
> negatively impacts the efficient
> operations of your public sector
> employer, you can legally be
> • disciplined/terminated.

CASE STUDY

A local firefighter is involved in an online debate with a stranger late at night. He has been drinking.

During the debate with strangers, an African-American women posts, "Black lives matter." The firefighter responds with what can only be described as a racist rant, with racial epithets and other highly offensive racist statements.

His public sector employer learns of the post and the firefighter is immediately terminated.

The firefighter apologizes, saying he was intoxicated and doesn't remember making the post.

What he did outside of work impacted his ability to work in his job.

CASE STUDY

During the Coronavirus pandemic, a man working at a law firm is upset with the mask mandate.

He posts on Twitter, "No more masks. Any business that tells me to put on a mask (Whole Foods on Lomo Alto) in Dallas will get told to kiss my Corona a** and will lose my business forever. It's time to stop this B***S**T. Do I have to show the lame security guard outside of a ghetto store my CV19 test results? I will show him my Glock 21 shooting range results. With Hornady hollow points. Pricey ammo, but worth it in this situation."

People begin tagging his employer on the post, complaining about the violent tone.

The employer announces the man is being terminated, stating **the post violated the firm's values** and the authorities have been notified.

CASE STUDY

A woman who works as a vice president for a television network engages in an online conversation about the Las Vegas shooting that occurred in 2017. She comments she doesn't have sympathy for the victims because they are Republicans.

She states, "If they wouldn't do anything when children were murdered, I have no hope that the Repugs will ever do the right thing. I'm actually not even sympathetic because country music fans often are Republican gun-toters."

Her employer terminates her.

She writes the following apology: "Earlier today I posted an indefensible post in a Facebook discussion thread concerning the tragic Las Vegas shooting, a statement I sincerely regret. I am deeply sorry for diminishing the significance of every life affected by Stephen Paddock's terrorism last night and for the pain my words have inflicted on the loved ones of the victims. My shameful comments do not reflect the beliefs of my former employer, colleagues, family, and friends. Nor do they reflect my actual beliefs. This senseless violence warrants the deepest empathy. I understand and accept all consequences that my words have incurred."

While her apology perhaps does some damage control, **she loses a great job over making an insensitive comment online.**

CASE STUDY

A female Twitter user is engaged in a direct message conversation with a newspaper reporter when he acknowledges an "awkward transition" by asking her if she thought about applying for reporter positions.

Then, with no prompting from the Twitter user, the reporter states, "Anyway, you're so beautiful." Three minutes later he messages, "Anyway, you are hilarious."

She does not respond to either message.

Forty minutes later he makes a sexual comment. She responds, "This isn't appropriate or acceptable."

He apologizes, saying it wasn't intended for her.

The Twitter user complains to the reporter's company. He resigns from his job for interacting in this manner with a member of the public.

Each of these examples shows a profound lack of good judgment and the foolish ending of a career over nonsense.

Before posting, texting, or engaging in any electronic communication, ask yourself:

- What's in it for me? Why am I sending/posting this?

- What if this was shared with the world—my mom, grandmother, siblings, a judge, a jury, my boss, coworkers, neighbors, my pastor, etc.?

- What's the worst that can happen?

When in doubt, don't send/post!

Ask yourself how the post/text can impact the following:

How could my conduct impact . . . ?

my ability to maintain public trust	my relationships with my peers & supervisors	my relationships with clients	my finances
my family	my freedom	my ability to be objective in my work	my ability to put my organization in the best light

TIP: It's 10:00 p.m. and you are on your third glass of wine/beer. **Get off the computer and your phone.** Most of these controversial posts occur when people are intoxicated and angry.

Your Rights: Private sector nonmanagement employees have a right to engage in concerted activity for their mutual aid and protection under Section 7 of the National Labor Relations Act.

This does not give you the right to vent about your job.

It gives you the right to engage in a conversation with other coworkers about working conditions.

This right is limited to certain situations. **Use caution when posting about your job** because it is unlikely this law will apply, as it narrowly includes only those situations where a person is speaking in concert with coworkers about general working conditions, not voicing a personal grievance.

Don't Be a Bully or a Jerk

Workplace bullying happens too often. Behaviors such as **verbal abuse, intimidation, and hostile conduct usually are signs of workplace bullying.**

Laws generally do not protect against workplace bullying, but it most likely violates your company's code of conduct or workplace violence policies.

Bullying can occur by managers toward subordinates, between coworkers, and by employees toward their managers.

CASE STUDY

Fred is a new employee and for some reason, people don't like him. Coworkers berate him, make him feel unwelcome, exclude him from team interactions and lunches, and generally try to embarrass and humiliate him as much as possible.

This amounts to workplace bullying.

CASE STUDY

Sally dislikes her coworker, so she ignores her, intentionally refuses to assist with work, and gossips about her so others won't like her.

This is how Sally maintains control. **This translates to being a workplace bully.**

If you are angry about something, don't be a jerk about it. **Be professional in resolving your problem.**

It's just work.
It's going to be OK.

Yelling or becoming abusive will make it worse, and you will probably lose your job.

Employees who feel they are being bullied at work need to speak up. Tell human resources, call the alert hotline if you have one, or tell someone in management.

There are many signs that you are being bullied at work. You may feel sick or dread coming to work, your family and friends notice a change in you, you are depressed or feel anxious all the time, and you start to lose your confidence or sense of self-worth. These signs should not be ignored. Try to get the support of coworkers who have witnessed the bullying and go together to report it to HR or management.

Your Rights at Work

Even though most employees are "at will," which means they can be fired for any reason or no reason at all, **employees cannot be fired for an illegal reason.**

In addition, employees enjoy certain legal rights in the workplace. The major federal laws are outlined in the next few pages, but you might also have state laws that apply.

! ● While there are many legal rights at work, there are also many activities that are not protected by federal law.

For example, you have no right under federal law to the following:

- Meal periods

- Breaks

- Paid leave

- Paid vacation

- Paid holidays

- Extra pay for weekend work

- Extra pay for working more than eight hours a day

- Extra pay for working a holiday

However, if you are provided those things voluntarily by your employer, there may be additional rights and rules applied to them.

For example, while you don't have a right to a break, if your employer offers one for less than 20 minutes you are entitled to be paid for that short break if you are an "hourly" or "nonexempt" employee.

Pay—Fair Labor Standards Act

If you are a nonexempt (hourly) worker, you have a right to be paid at least the federal minimum wage (or the state wage, if higher) and to be paid for *all* hours worked.

You are also entitled to receive overtime at time and a half of your regular rate of pay for all hours worked over 40 in a work week. **This right cannot be waived.**

If your employer provides an unpaid meal period of 30 minutes or more, and you work through lunch, you have a right to be paid for that time.

You can make up the time during the same workweek but not in subsequent workweeks.

CASE STUDY

You are a receptionist and you take lunch at your desk, but you are still expected to greet customers and answer the phone during this time. Even if the phone doesn't ring and no guests arrive for you to greet, **you are "engaged to wait," and you are entitled by federal law to be paid for that time.**

CASE STUDY

You respond to personal calls a few times during the workday. Your manager makes you clock out each time these calls occur, which are about 10 minutes each.

Your manager has violated federal law. You are not entitled to any breaks or meal periods by federal law (some states require it) but if you do get a break, short breaks of 20 minutes or less are compensable (meaning you cannot have your pay withheld for this time).

CASE STUDY

Only meal periods of around 30 minutes or more count toward unpaid time. Meal periods must be uninterrupted.

If you start your lunch break at noon, and you are interrupted by 15 minutes from 12:15 p.m. to 12:30 p.m., you don't get the balance of the 30 minutes. The clock restarts.

You are either paid for your meal period at this point *or* your meal period now starts at 12:30 p.m. and will go until 1:00 p.m.

You should only dock yourself 30 minutes on your timesheet. That first 15 minutes is too short to count as a meal period.

CASE STUDY

You work really hard on a project this week and work 50 hours.

Your employer tells you to make it up next week and only work 30 hours the subsequent week, since it is all within the same pay period.

It would be illegal for the employer to pay you for 80 hours of straight pay in this scenario.

You are entitled to 10 hours of overtime from the previous week and 30 hours of straight pay in the subsequent week.

If you work in the public sector, you may be entitled to compensatory time off at one-and-a-half times the overtime you worked. However, certain restrictions apply. The private sector cannot provide "comp time."

> **!** Note that some industries like police, fire, and others have special rules. More information can be found at: **www.dol.gov/whd.**

Harassment and Discrimination

Under federal discrimination laws, if you work for an employer with 15 or more employees, **you have a right to not be discriminated against or harassed** based on protected characteristics to include the following:

- Title VII of the Civil Rights Act of 1964

Race

Gender
(including sex and sexual harassment,
sexual orientation, gender identity)

Color

National origin

Religion

- Pregnancy (Pregnancy Discrimination Act)

- Disability (Americans with Disabilities Act)

- Genetic information (Genetic Information Nondiscrimination Act)

If you work for an employer with 20 or more employees, you may be entitled to protections against age discrimination/harassment:

- Age (age 40 and over)
  (Age Discrimination in Employment Act)

> Employers cannot make a
> hiring or any employment
> decision based on any
> of these protected
> characteristics.

You have a right to be free from a hostile work environment based on these protected characteristics or be subjected to quid-pro-quo harassment. You should never have to come to work and be subjected to conduct based on these protections.

> **!** Employees are entitled to reasonable accommodation for their disabilities and/or sincerely held religious beliefs, but to receive an accommodation, the employee must request one.

While only employers with 15 or more employees must comply with federal employment discrimination laws, **many states provide rights equal to or greater than those provided by federal law** and also require employers with less than 15 employees to comply with certain state anti-discrimination laws. These rights can change annually with each state's legislative session.

According to the Equal Employment Opportunity Commission ("EEOC"), harassment is unwelcome conduct that is based on a protected characteristic.

> "Harassment becomes unlawful where
> 1) enduring the offensive conduct becomes a condition of continued employment, or
> 2) the conduct is severe or pervasive enough to create a work environment that a reasonable person would consider intimidating, hostile, or abusive."

The EEOC also notes:

> "Petty slights, annoyances, and isolated incidents (unless extremely serious) will not rise to the level of illegality. To be unlawful, the conduct must create a work environment that would be intimidating, hostile, or offensive to reasonable people."

While you have a right to not be harassed—don't be offended by every petty slight.

The EEOC identifies offensive conduct that could rise to the level of harassment as:

"offensive jokes, slurs, epithets or name calling, physical assaults or threats, intimidation, ridicule or mockery, insults or put-downs, offensive objects or pictures, and interference with work performance."

Don't wait for something to build up to the point of illegal harassment. Speak up early, not just for yourself, but for others that may be experiencing harassment or discrimination.

In most states, the state antidiscrimination laws are enforced by the state's office of attorney general or by a state human rights division. In addition, some localities have their own Fair Employment Practices division. You can find these resources online through your state or local websites.

CASE STUDY

A customer becomes angry with your employee and calls her a racial slur.

The employee has a right to come to work and not have to endure this racial harassment by anyone, including customers.

The employee should tell his or her manager or human resources so the customer can be put on notice, indicating such conduct will not be tolerated.

You should consult your employee handbook or policies to learn how best to have your concerns addressed. It may be human resources, management, an alert or hotline, or all of the above.

> **!** You should never have to tell the person who is engaging in the misconduct in order to have your complaint addressed.

You have a right to not be retaliated against for bringing your complaint forward.

CASE STUDY

Alice's manager continues to make creepy comments, get too close to her, and ask her questions that are too personal and make her uncomfortable. She hesitates to tell anyone for fear that she will not be believed or that she will suffer retaliation.

The laws are designed to protect victims and those that bring these issues forward. **You must speak up if you want the behaviors to stop.**

More information can be found at **www.eeoc.gov.**

Medical Leave and Medical Accommodations

Family Medical Leave Act (FMLA)

To receive benefits under the FMLA, **you must work for a "covered employer."** These include the following:

- Private sector employers with 50 or more employees

- Public agencies, including local, state, or federal government agencies, regardless of the number of employees it employs

- Public or private elementary or secondary school, regardless of the number of employees it employs

Under the FMLA, if you work for a covered employer, **you are entitled to up to 12 workweeks in a 12-month period of unpaid leave** if you meet the following criteria:

- Work for a company with at least 50 or more employees located within a 75-mile radius of your workplace

- Have worked for the company at least 12 months (cumulative, not consecutive)

- Have worked at least 1,250 hours in the preceding 12 months

You may be eligible for the benefit for the following reasons:

- The birth of a child and to care for the newborn child within one year of birth

- The placement of a child with you for adoption or foster care and to care for the newly placed child within one year of placement

- To care for your spouse, child, or parent who has a serious health condition

- Your own serious health condition that makes you unable to perform the essential functions of your job

- Any qualifying exigency arising from your spouse, son, daughter, or parent as a covered military member on covered active duty

Serious Health Condition

A serious health condition includes inpatient care, continuing treatment (more than three days of incapacity), pregnancy or prenatal care, chronic conditions, permanent or long-term conditions, or multiple treatments.

You are entitled to return to the same, or equivalent, position at the conclusion of your leave. Your health care coverage must not be impacted, as long as you continue to pay your portion of the premiums during your leave.

Leave can be taken continuously
(all 12 weeks at a time)
or intermittently
(in some cases one hour at a time).

To qualify for FMLA, **you will need to advise your employer of your need for time off** due to one of these conditions. You will receive paperwork to be completed by your medical provider or the medical provider of your spouse, child, or parent.

> **!** Note that the leave is unpaid, but you typically will, and in some cases may be required to, use your paid leave (PTO, sick time, etc.) that will run concurrently with your FMLA.

This will enable you to be paid for the time off, but you will be cutting into your paid time off and you may not be able to take a vacation later in the year if you've used up all of your paid time off. **You must submit the completed paperwork to qualify for the benefit.**

Covered Service Member Leave

You may also be entitled to up to 26 workweeks of leave during a single 12-month period to care for a covered service member with a serious injury or illness if the eligible employee is the service member's spouse, son, daughter, parent, or next of kin. Several restrictions apply.

For more information, you should talk to your HR department. To learn more, you can also go to: https://www.dol.gov/whd/fmla/.

Americans with Disabilities Act (ADA)

The ADA gives eligible applicants and employees who work for an employer with 15 or more employees the right to reasonable accommodations in the workplace due to a record of or an actual disability, unless it would cause your employer an undue hardship.

> A disability, under the ADA, is a mental or physical impairment that substantially limits one or more life activities or bodily functions.

These include diabetes, severe back issues, depression, major medical conditions, and injuries.

Disabled employees are also entitled to be free from harassment or discrimination due to their disability or for being regarded as having a disability, even if they don't actually have one.

> **!** Reasonable accommodations can include a change in the method or manner in which the work is performed (i.e., some employers require a retail cashier to stand but due to a disability, the employee may be entitled to use a chair to perform the job).

It can also include special equipment, such as a large monitor or special keyboard.

Unpaid leave can also be a reasonable accommodation, but **generally, leave pursuant to the ADA cannot be indefinite or sporadic.** There is no specific time limit for leave as a reasonable accommodation like the FMLA.

The employer and the employee should work together to determine what reasonable accommodations can be offered to enable the employee to peform the essential function of the job.

An employee needing a reasonable accommodation should first tell his/her manager or HR that, due to a medical condition, a reasonable accommodation is needed.

> **The ADA is prospective, not retrospective.** Once you are being disciplined or fired for performance or behavior, it is too late to tell your employer you need a reasonable accommodation.

If you are not able to do your job because of your disability and need an accommodation, speak up early. **The employer is not obligated to provide any accommodation until you request one.**

The reasonable accommodation discussion includes an "**interactive process**," where you will explain your needs and may be asked to provide medical documentation.

Management and usually the human resources department will then determine whether a reasonable accommodation can be provided. Employees needing an accommodation do not always get the accommodation they want.

> **!** The employer only needs to provide an accommodation that is effective to assist the employee to perform the essential functions of the job.

Reasonable accommodations are never an excuse to lower performance standards or to take away essential job functions. It is not a shield to avoid discipline or doing the job fully.

For example, if the job requires that you make 15 widgets a day, it is not a reasonable accommodation to allow you to produce only 13 widgets a day. A reasonable accommodation would be giving you a tool to help you achieve the job requirement of 15 widgets a day.

More information can be found at:
https://www.eeoc.gov/laws/types/disability.cfm

Workers' Compensation

Worker's compensation is governed by state law. Your employer will pay for the insurance coverage of worker's compensation insurance.

You don't need to do anything to get coverage.

If you suffer an injury while working that arises out of or in the course of employment, you will likely be eligible for paid time off at a reduced amount after a waiting period. Your associated medical bills will also be paid.

You may also be covered if you are exposed to chemicals or other toxins at work that causes you to become ill.

You may not get coverage if your injury resulted from a violation of a safety rule **where you knew the rule.**

Always follow all safety rules!

No matter how small the injury, you should **report all injuries** to HR or to the worker's compensation carrier. Typically, employers will publish where to report a workplace injury.

! You cannot be retaliated against for filing a worker's compensation claim.

Religious Accommodations

In addition to the nondiscrimination and harassment rights for religion, you are entitled to receive reasonable accommodations for your religious beliefs as long as you work for an employer with 15 or more employees and you have a sincerely held religious belief.

If you need a religious accommodation, you need to ask for an accommodation from human resources or your manager.

You will then engage in an interactive discussion to identify accommodations that might be effective and reasonable.

The company is not required to provide an accommodation if doing so creates an undue hardship (such as inadequate staffing).

CASE STUDY

A health care center in Texas is ordered to pay $375,000 to 10 former employees following a lawsuit filed against it for religious discrimination and harassment by the Equal Employment Opportunity Commission.

The lawsuit alleged that the health care company conducted mandatory meetings each morning that involved prayer and reading of biblical verses, "including discussion of how those principles applied to the employees' personal lives."

CASE STUDY

An employee who follows the principles of Buddhism asks her employer several times to be excused from attending the religious portion of the daily staff meeting as a reasonable accommodation for her religion. The employer denies her request, and she is terminated.

Employees have a right to not be pressured to engage in religious-based activities, including meetings, social events, conversations, and prayers unless that person works for a religious organization (a very limited exception in the law).

The EEOC's Compliance Manual on Religious Discrimination provides six specific practices that violate Title VII's prohibition on religious discrimination:

- Treating applicants or employees differently by taking an adverse action based on their religious beliefs, observances or practices (or lack of religious beliefs, observances or practices) in any aspect of employment.

- Taking adverse action motivated by a desire to avoid accommodating a religious belief, observance or practice that the employer knew or suspected may be needed and would not pose an undue hardship.

- Denying a needed reasonable accommodation sought for an applicant's or employee's sincerely held religious beliefs, observances or practices if an accommodation will not impose an undue hardship on the conduct of the business.

- Intentionally limiting, segregating or classifying employees based on the presence or absence of religious beliefs, observances or practices or enforcing a neutral rule that would have the same effect and cannot be justified by business necessity.

- Subjecting employees to harassment because of their religious beliefs, observances or practices (or lack of religious beliefs, observances or practices).

- Retaliating against an applicant or employee who has opposed discrimination on the basis of religion, or participated in any manner in an investigation, proceeding or hearing regarding discrimination on the basis of religion.

The compliance manual and more information can be found at EEOC.gov.

Military Leave

The Uniformed Services Employment and Re-employment Rights Act (USERRA) **protects members of the military reserve in their rights to serve the military when activated and attend other necessary trainings and events.**

All employers, regardless of size, must comply with this law.

Covered members have reemployment rights.

This means you have a right to be reemployed in your civilian job if you leave that job to perform service in the uniformed service. To qualify you must

- Give your employer advance written or verbal notice of your service;
- Spent five or less years of cumulative service in the uniformed service with this employer;
- Comply with timely return to work notifications; and
- You have not been separated from service with a disqualifying discharge or under other than honorable conditions.

NOTE: If you are eligible to be reemployed, you must be restored to the job and benefits you would have attained if you had not been absent due to military service or, in some cases, a comparable job.

You also have a right to be free from discrimination and retaliation.

If you:

- are a past or present member of the uniformed service;
- have applied for membership in the uniformed service; or
- are obligated to serve in the uniformed service.

You also have a right to health insurance protection.

More information can be found at **https://www.dol.gov/vets/programs/userra/.**

Safe Workplace

Pursuant to the Occupational Safety & Health Administration (OSHA), **all employees have a right to a safe workplace,** free of known health and safety hazards.

According to OSHA, you have a right to the following:

- Be trained in a language you understand

- Work on machines that are safe

- Access to required safety gear, such as gloves or a harness and lifeline for falls

- Be protected from toxic chemicals

- Request an OSHA inspection and speak to the inspector

- Report an injury or illness and get copies of your medical records

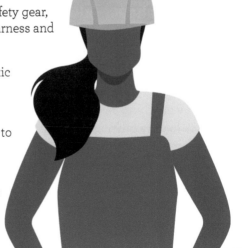

- See copies of the workplace injury and illness log
- Review records of work-related injuries and illnesses
- Get copies of test results done to find hazards in the workplace

> You also have a right to complain about safety concerns without fear of retaliation.

With the COVID-19 pandemic, some states, the Centers for Disease Control, and OSHA provided guidance, and in some cases, mandated certain safety standards to protect workers from contracting the virus.

You should follow all the safety standards set by your employer.

You should also advocate for improved safety conditions if you feel unsafe.

Guidelines are being updated regularly, and your employer will want to keep you and others safe, so speak up if you see anything causes you concern, whether COVID-related or for any other safety issue .

More information can be found at: **www.osha.gov.**

Closing

Working can bring a tremendous amount of personal satisfaction.

You might not get told on a regular basis that you have done a good job. You might not be told you are valued at work.

Not every manager does a good job at showing appreciation for the very people that add value to the organization's success. While not ideal to feel dismissed in this way, **do not let other people determine your worth.**

Answer to yourself. Determine what you expect out of yourself. Set and evaluate your own goals.

Hold yourself accountable for achieving your goals. Don't blame others or become easily agitated over small or petty slights.

Working is a signficant part of our lives and livelihood. By taking the advice in this book, you will be well on your way to an amazing career and you will STAY HIRED—not fired!

! You are in control of your own destiny, so take charge and conquer every single workday.

About the Author

 Karen Michael, Esq. is the President of KarenMichael, PLC, an employment law and human resources consulting firm specializing in workplace investigations, management and leadership training, and HR and legal advice.

After spending three decades advising organizations on employment matters as a practicing employment attorney, HR executive and HR Consultant, Karen discovered the missing piece to a respectful and legally compliant workplace starts with setting expectations from the beginning with employees. The last thing an employer wants to do is fire an employee, and much energy and time is spent talking about employee issues. To solve this, Karen has combined her years of experience in working with organizations to compile the specific behaviors of a successful employee and to explain the legal rights of employees in the workplace.

Karen is a sought after national speaker on HR-related topics and writes a weekly labor law column on workplace issues. Readers can rely upon her expert advice in a easy-to-read explanation of specific behaviors you need to stay hired, not fired.

For more information about Karen and her services can be found at www.karenmichaelconsulting.com